TRANSPORTATION ADVENTURES

Written by
Doug Barone

ON THE SEA

KidHaven
PUBLISHING

Published in 2027 by
KidHaven Publishing, an Imprint of Greenhaven Publishing, LLC
2544 Clinton St., Buffalo, NY 14224

Written by: Doug Barone
Edited by: Rebecca Phillips-Bartlett
Designed by: Ker Ker Lee

Cataloging-in-Publication Data

Names: Barone, Doug.
Title: On the sea / Doug Barone.
Description: Buffalo, NY : KidHaven Publishing, 2027. | Series: Transportation adventures | Includes glossary and index.
Identifiers: ISBN 9781534569713 (pbk.) | ISBN 9781534569720 (library bound) | ISBN 9781534569737 (ebook)
Subjects: LCSH: Boats and boating--Juvenile literature. | Ships--Juvenile literature. | Cruise ships--Juvenile literature. | Jet skiing--Juvenile literature.
Classification: LCC VM150.B376 2027 | DDC 623.82--dc23

Printed in China

CPSIA compliance information: Batch #QS27KH: For further information contact Greenhaven Publishing LLC at 1-844-317-7404.

Please visit our website, www.greenhavenpublishing.com.
For a free color catalog of all our high-quality books, call toll free 1-844-317-7404 or fax 1-844-317-7405.

Find us on

Photo Credits – Images courtesy of Shutterstock.com, unless otherwise stated.

Cover & Recurring – muratart, freevideophotoagency. 2–3 – Olesia Bilkei. 4–5 – ronstik, stockphoto mania. 6–7 – KOTOIMAGES, spatuletail. 8–9 – Nowaczyk, xbrchx. 10–11 – docent, Mariusz Niedzwiedzki, TamuT. 12–13 – GreenOak, Aerial-motion. 14–15 – GreenOak. 16–17 – Thomas D Dittmer, Philip Bird LRPS CPAGB, Ella Miller. 18–19 – koonsiri boonnak, AlexDreamliner. 20–21 – wavebreakmedia, Studio Peace. 22–23 – anek.soowannaphoom, Dreamer Company.

CONTENTS

Words that look like this can be found in the glossary on page 24.

GOING ON AN ADVENTURE!

Transportation is how we take trips. Different forms of transportation can take you different places. You might travel to the store or to a different country!

ON THE SEA

People have been crossing the seas for thousands of years. Even swimming counts as a form of transportation. Most people travel across the water using boats. Have you ever been on a boat?

ROWBOATS

The earliest boats date back to ancient history. The ancient Egyptians made boats out of reeds. People used wooden poles or oars to push the boats through the water. This is called rowing.

Today, many people still use rowboats. Some people use rowboats for exercise. Others use rowboats for racing across the water. Rowing is a sport!

SAILBOATS

A sail is a large piece of material that catches the wind. On boats, sails are attached to poles called masts. Catching the wind pushes the boat through the water.

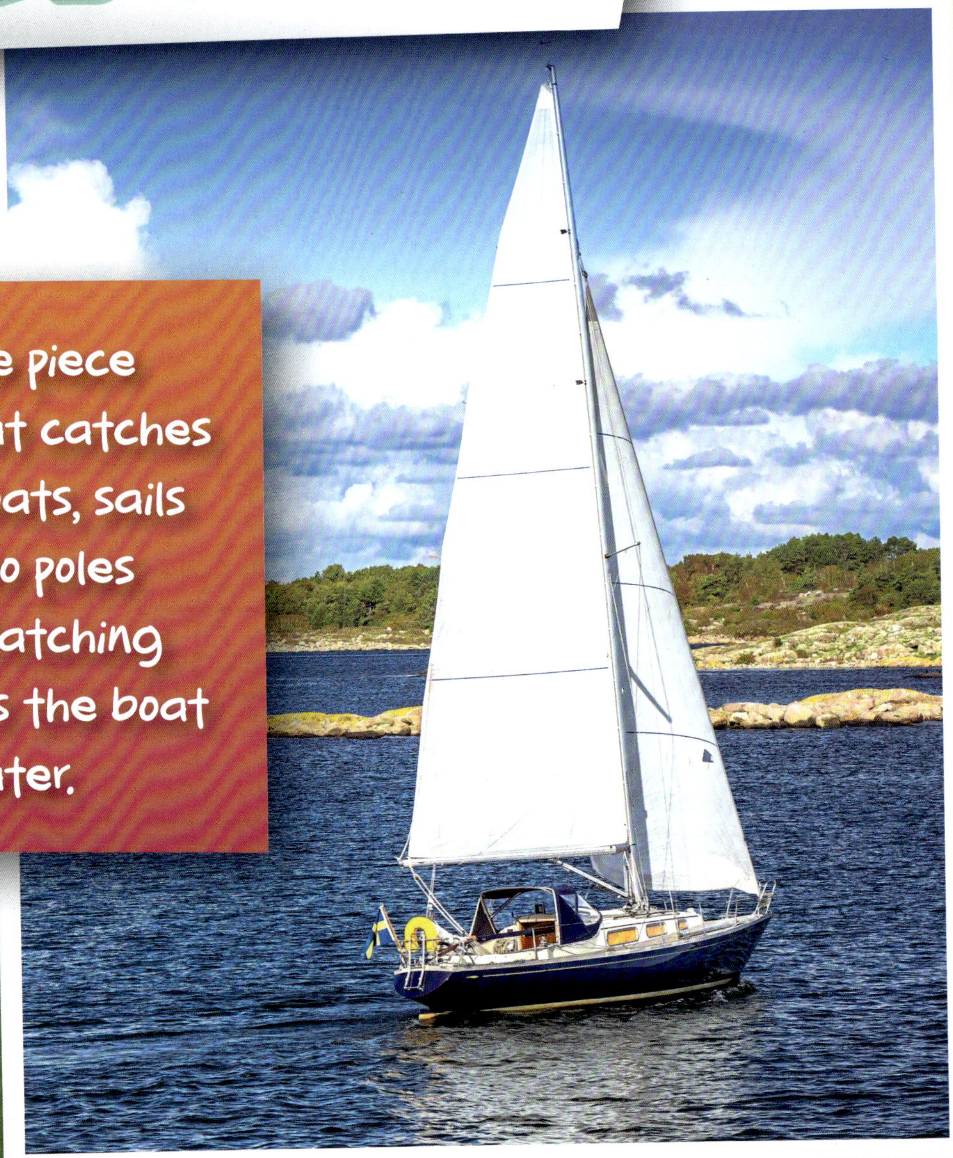

The Vikings were known for their sailboats. The boats the Vikings used are known as longships. They used longships to travel across the sea from Europe to Greenland to North America.

STEAMBOATS

People began working with steam engines in the 1700s CE. Steamboats use steam engines to power a paddle wheel. The wheel spins and pushes the boat through the water.

Early paddle wheel steamboats did not work very well on rough water. So, larger steamboats, which use propellers instead of wheels, were invented. These boats are better suited to the choppy ocean waters.

propeller

CARGO SHIPS

Goods often need to be carried overseas. Lots of goods are transported on cargo ships. Different kinds of cargo ships transport different kinds of goods.

Some cargo ships are made to transport liquids.

Some cargo ships are made to transport chemicals.

Some cargo ships transport large containers. These containers can hold goods such as clothes and food. The containers can be stacked on top of each other.

CRUISE SHIPS

Cruise ships are a mode of transportation used by people going on vacation. Cruise ships take their passengers to exciting places around the world.

Where would you go on a cruise ship?

Cruise ships can be huge and can carry a lot of passengers. They have many things for people to do as they travel. There might be restaurants, shops, and swimming pools on the ship.

SPEEDBOATS

Speedboats are small boats that are designed to get around quickly. Their powerful engines let them reach high speeds on the water. Speedboats can be a fun way to explore the sea.

Speedboats can be used for waterskiing. The person wearing the skis needs to hold on tight!

Police and fire departments use speedboats when there are emergencies at sea. These boats are very useful!

JET SKIS

Jet Skis are some of the smallest vehicles used to travel across the sea. They can usually only carry one or two passengers at a time.

Jet Skis tend to be used for a fun time on the water rather than getting from place to place. Their engines help them reach high speeds for a thrilling ride.

THE FUTURE ON THE SEA

People have been coming up with new modes of transportation for thousands of years. There are still people hard at work coming up with new ways to travel across the sea.

What would you invent to explore the sea?

Jetboards and water jet packs have become more popular in recent years. Maybe one day, everyone will be using jet packs to get across the ocean.

Would you try these modes of transportation?

TRANSPORTATION ADVENTURES

There are lots of vehicles to take on the water. If it is too far to swim, you can speed by on a Jet Ski or relax on a cruise ship!

There are lots of different ways to have an adventure on the sea. Which vehicles have you ridden on? Which one do you want to try next?

GLOSSARY

ancient	belonging to the very distant past
chemicals	substances that are usually made or used by scientists
liquids	materials that flow, such as water
oars	poles with flat blades that are used to row or steer boats
reeds	tall, thin plants that are like grass
steam engines	machines that use the gas made from heating water to power things
vehicles	machines that are used to carry people or things

INDEX